Better Homes and Gardens®

LET'S GO EXPLORING

First Edition. First Printing.
Library of Congress Catalog Card Number: 90-63296
ISBN: 0-696-01933-7

Inside You'll Find...

The Wonderful Woods

Max likes to go exploring in the woods. Each time he discovers something new. Today, he finds a neighborhood of animal homes. The snail carries his home on his back. Can you think of other animals that live in their own shells?

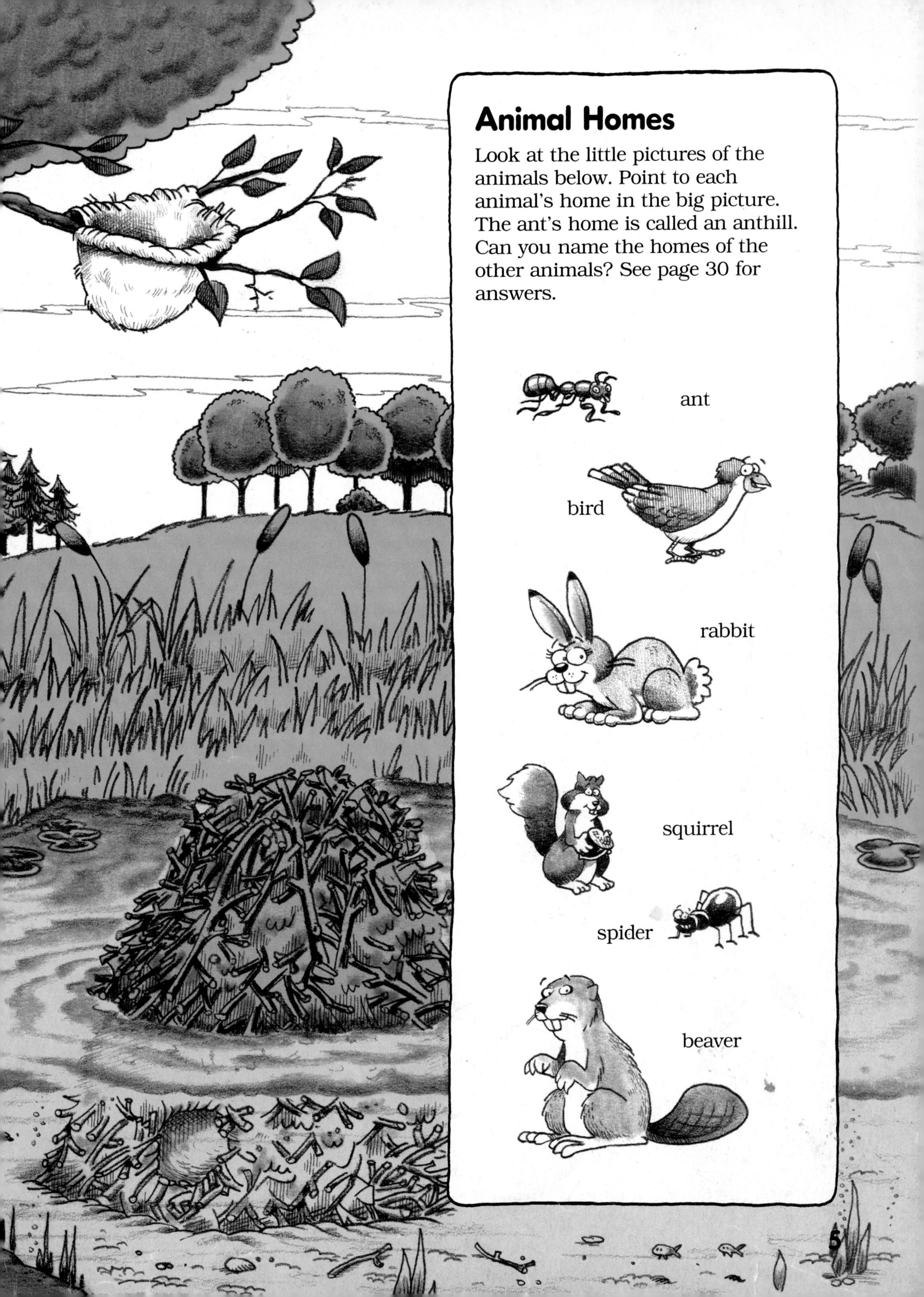

Animal Homes

Look at the little pictures of the animals below. Point to each animal's home in the big picture. The ant's home is called an anthill. Can you name the homes of the other animals? See page 30 for answers.

Woodsy Picture Frame

Make your favorite drawing or photograph extra special by framing it. Finding the twigs for your frame is half the fun of framing your picture. Search for the twigs in your backyard or a nearby park.

What you'll need...

- Scissors
- Ruler
- One 9x12-inch sheet of construction paper
- One 5x7-inch drawing or photograph (see page 30)
- Tape
- 4 twigs
- White crafts glue

1 Cut four 1-inch-wide strips from the construction paper. Place 1 strip on the work surface. Place the drawing upside down on 1 lengthwise edge of the strip. Tape the drawing to the strip (see photo).

Repeat with the remaining strips and sides of the drawing. The strips will be longer than your drawing.

2 Turn the drawing over. Cut off the long ends of the construction paper strips to make a rectangle (see photo).

3 Break 2 twigs so they are the same length as the 2 short sides of the rectangle. Break the remaining 2 twigs so they are the same length as the 2 long sides of the rectangle.

Put some glue along the edge of each construction paper strip. The glue lines need to be thick. Stick the twigs on the glue (see photo). Let dry.

Cinnamon Snail Snacks

Hiking in the woods makes Max hungry. Here's a lip-smacking snail-shaped snack he likes to make from bread and cream cheese.

What you'll need...

- Table knife
- 4 slices soft-textured bread
- ¼ cup soft-style cream cheese
- 2 mixing bowls
- 3 tablespoons sugar
- 1½ teaspoons ground cinnamon
- Spoon
- ¼ cup melted margarine or butter
- Cookie sheet
- Hot pads
- Foil

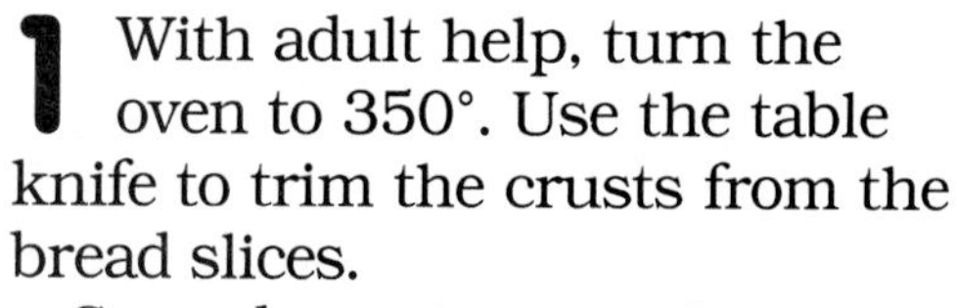

1 With adult help, turn the oven to 350°. Use the table knife to trim the crusts from the bread slices.

Spread some cream cheese on each slice of bread. Roll up the bread slices with the cream cheese on the inside (see photo). Cut each slice into three rolls.

2 In 1 of the bowls mix the sugar and the cinnamon with the spoon.

Put the melted margarine in the other bowl. Dip each roll into the melted margarine (see photo). Then, put the roll in the sugar-cinnamon mixture. Coat the bread portion with sugar-cinnamon mixture. Be sure not to coat the cream cheese.

3 Place rolls on a cookie sheet (see photo).

With adult help, bake in a 350° oven about 12 minutes or till light brown and crisp.

Use hot pads to remove the rolls from the oven. Cool them about 15 minutes before eating. Wrap leftovers in foil and put them in the refrigerator. Makes 12 snacks.

Snail Snack Fillings

Here are more ideas for yummy fillings:

- Use soft-style cream cheese with strawberry or pineapple.
- Sprinkle the cream cheese with raisins before you roll up the bread slices.
- Spread the cream cheese with jelly before you roll up the bread slices.

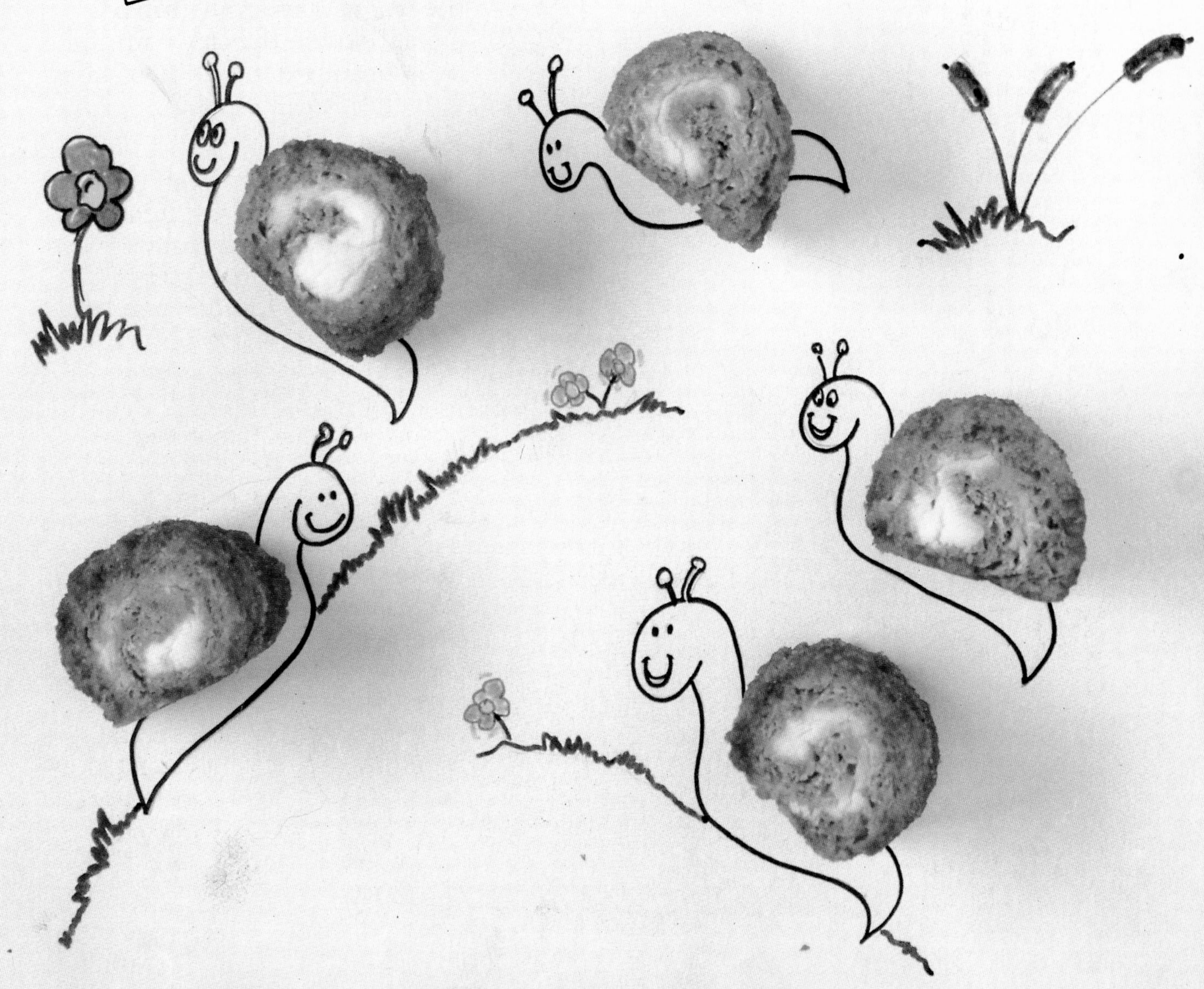

Leaf Knickknack

Have you ever heard of a knickknack? It's a pretty little object that makes you feel good. This knickknack helps you remember the beauty of summertime leaves all year long.

What you'll need...

- Tape
- Waxed paper
- Homemade Clay (see page 30)
- Plastic wrap or one 1-pint heavy-duty sealable plastic bag
- Ruler
- Leaf (see tip on page 11)
- Markers, water colors, or tempera paints

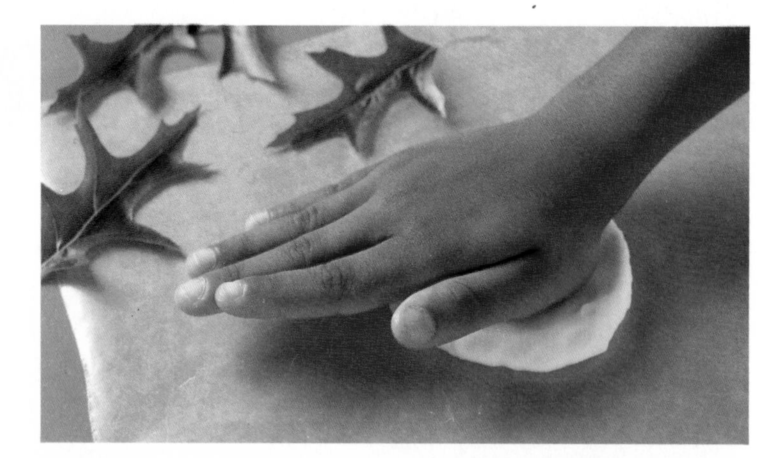

1 Tape a piece of waxed paper to your work surface. Break off a fistful of Homemade Clay. To store the remaining clay, tightly wrap it in plastic wrap and keep in the refrigerator.

Roll the clay into a ball. Place the ball of clay on the waxed paper. Flatten the clay with the palm of your hand till it is about ½ inch thick (see photo).

2 Place a leaf on top of the clay. Press the leaf into the clay (see photo). Carefully remove the leaf. Put the leaf imprint on a wire rack and let it dry overnight.

3 Use markers to color the leaf imprint any way you like (see photo).

Use your Leaf Knickknack as a decoration for a shelf in your room or as a gift for a special friend.

Look for These Leaves

Although any leaf will work for this project, some leaves make a better imprint than others. Maple, oak, and fern leaves are good choices.

Be sure to ask a parent's permission before you pick leaves off a tree.

Mountain Adventures

Brrr! Max is getting ready to swoosh down the mountain on his skis, but his head, hands, and feet are cold. What does Max need to find before he starts down the mountain? To help Max, see the box on page 13.

Hidden Ski Gear

Look at the small picture of Max. How is Max different from the big picture above? He has all his ski gear in the small picture. Find the items Max is missing. They are hidden in the big picture.

The hidden items are 2 mittens, 2 skis, 2 ski poles, 2 ski boots, 1 hat, and 1 muffler.

Mud Mountain

Have you ever squished and squeezed mud between your fingers? That's exactly what you do when you mold Homemade Mud into a mountain. Most mountains in the world have names, so after you decorate your creation, name it. Max calls his creation Mount Max.

What you'll need...

- Homemade Mud (see page 31)
- 1 plastic-foam meat tray or paper plate
- Cotton balls
- Small stones, twigs, and leaves (see tip on page 15)
- Scissors
- 1 small piece of construction paper
- Tape
- 1 toothpick

1 Break off a fistful of Homemade Mud and place it on the meat tray. Use your hands to shape it into a mountain.

Break off more mud. Place it on top of the mountain (see photo). Use your hands to smooth the new mud into the mountain. Repeat till you have used all the Homemade Mud.

2 For snow, stretch the cotton ball till you have a thin layer of cotton. Place the snow on the mountain top (see photo). Put some stones around the bottom of the mountain.

For the flag, cut a small rectangle from the construction paper. Tape the rectangle to the toothpick. Stick the flag into the mountain top. Let dry.

Mountain Landscaping

To create a mountain scene, gather small stones and small twigs or leaves from your backyard. Arrange the stones around your mountain. For a tree, press an end of a twig or the stem of a leaf into the meat tray.

Skis and Snow

Imagine skiing down a mountain or across a field of snow, feeling the wind on your cheeks and the cold snowflakes on your nose. If that sounds like fun, make this little pair of skis and put them in a field of cotton-ball snow. Then, pretend some more.

What you'll need...

- 1 snap fastener
- White crafts glue
- 2 toothpicks
- 2 crafts sticks
- Cotton balls or polyester fiberfill
- One 6-inch paper plate

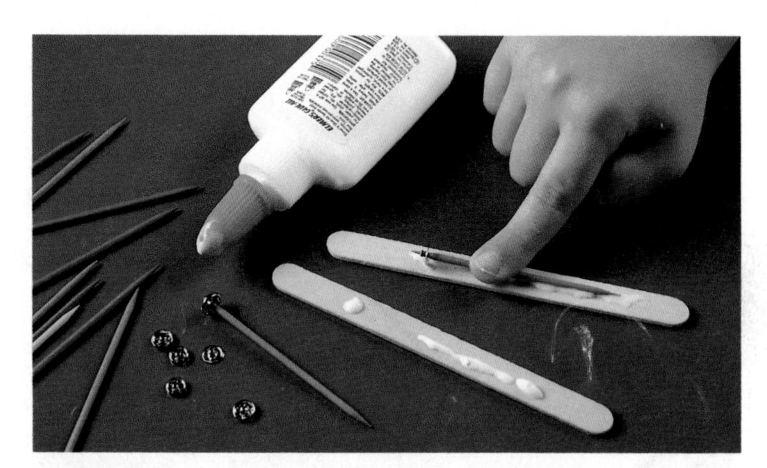

1 Unfasten the snap so you have 2 halves. For the ski poles, put some glue on the end of each toothpick. Push each toothpick through the hole in the center of 1 half of the snap.

Apply a small amount of glue to the crafts sticks. Place 1 pole on the glue on each crafts stick (see photo).

2 For snow, apply glue to the paper plate. Stick cotton balls onto the glue. Place the skis on top of the cotton.

Ski-Time Cocoa Mix

After skiing, Max warms his tummy with this yummy cocoa. For the mix, stir together 2½ cups *nonfat dry milk powder,* 1 cup *powdered sugar,* and ½ cup *unsweetened cocoa powder.* Put in an airtight container. For 1 serving, mix ⅓ cup of mix and ⅔ cup *water.* With adult help, heat well.

Desert Fun

After a morning of horseback riding, Max and Elliot stop to give their horses a drink of water. Elliot eats lunch, while Max searches for desert animals. Can you help Max find 6 lizards hidden in the picture?

Max and Elliot decide to play a word game. You can play, too. Point to the objects in the picture that begin with the letter S. Here are the objects:

- sun
- snake
- saddle
- sandwich
- sack
- spider
- shirt
- sunglasses
- sign
- spurs

Sew-and-Stuff Cactus

Pretend you are on a trip to the desert. Imagine the hot sun on your skin and the burning sand under your feet. Picture a cactus. It can be pointy or round. Now, make a paper cactus like the one you imagined finding in the desert.

What you'll need...

- Crayons, markers, or colored pencils
- Two 9x12-inch sheets of green construction paper
- Tape
- Scissors
- Paper punch
- Ruler
- Ribbon or yarn
- 2 or 3 paper towels

1 Draw a cactus on 1 sheet of paper. Place the drawing on top of the other sheet of paper. Tape the sheets together. Cut out the cactus drawing. Now you have 2 cactus shapes.

Place 1 cactus shape on top of the other. Use the paper punch to punch holes around the top and side (see photo). Do not punch holes along the bottom.

2 Cut a 12-inch piece of ribbon. Tape 1 end of the ribbon to the bottom of the cactus shape. Thread the ribbon through the nearest hole. Then, lace the ribbon through the remaining holes (see photo).

If you run out of ribbon, start over with another piece. Tape all loose ends of ribbon to the cactus.

3 If you like, draw designs on your cactus.

Tear the paper towels into small pieces. Push the paper towel pieces, 1 at a time, into the bottom of the cactus (see photo). Add paper towels until no more will fit.

Rigatoni Rattlesnake

Listen! Hear the snake rattle its tail. But don't be afraid. This friendly rattlesnake has popcorn in its tail and pasta tubes for scales.

What you'll need...

- Crayons or markers
- Construction paper
- Scissors
- One 25-inch-long piece of ribbon
- Tape
- Uncooked rigatoni or dyed rigatoni (see page 32)
- Rattlesnake Tail (see page 32)
- 10 kernels of unpopped popcorn

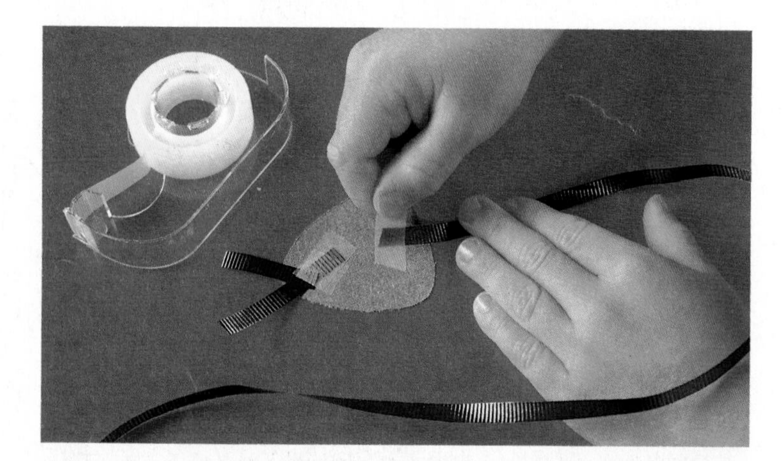

1 For the head, draw an egg shape on the construction paper. Cut out. Draw eyes on the head. Place the head facedown on your work surface.

For the tongue, cut 2 short pieces from the ribbon. Tape the 2 short pieces of ribbon to the narrow end of the head. Tape the long piece of ribbon to the wide end of the head (see photo).

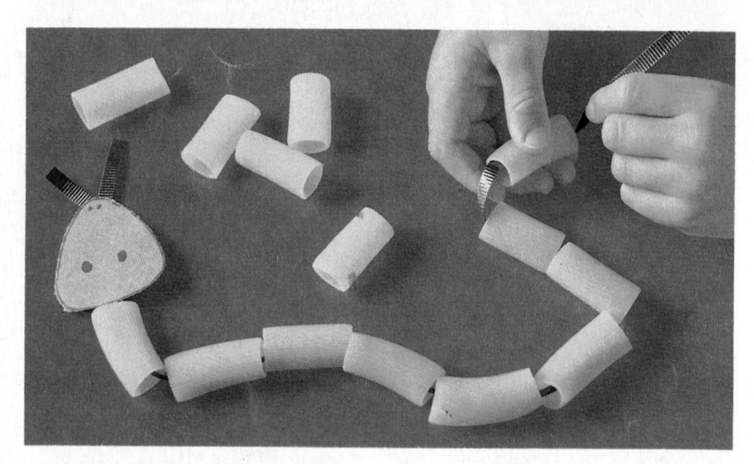

2 Thread the ribbon through a piece of rigatoni. Push the rigatoni piece to the head. Continue to thread rigatoni pieces on the ribbon till the ribbon is almost full (see photo).

3 Fold the Rattlesnake Tail on the fold lines. Unfold the tail. Put the popcorn in the center section of the tail. Fold the tail on the lines, overlapping the sides to cover the popcorn (see photo). Tape shut. Fold the straight unfolded side of the tail up toward the point. Tape shut. Tape the folded edge of the tail to the end of the ribbon.

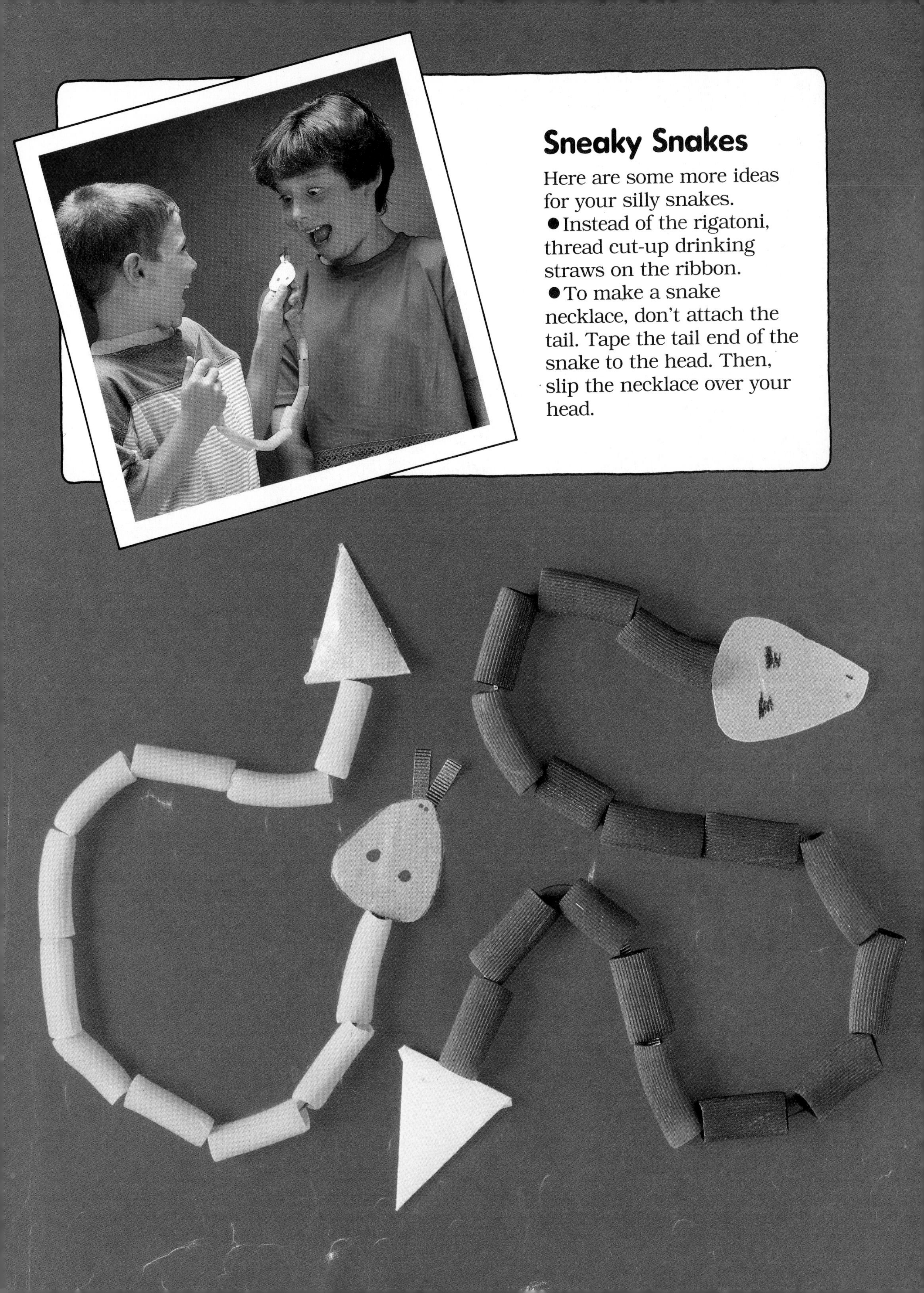

Sneaky Snakes

Here are some more ideas for your silly snakes.

- Instead of the rigatoni, thread cut-up drinking straws on the ribbon.
- To make a snake necklace, don't attach the tail. Tape the tail end of the snake to the head. Then, slip the necklace over your head.

Lake Pals

The turtle below wants to join her turtle and fish friends swimming in the lake. Trace the path she should take to the lake. Watch out for the trouble spots. Then, count the turtles in the lake. How many fish are in the lake?

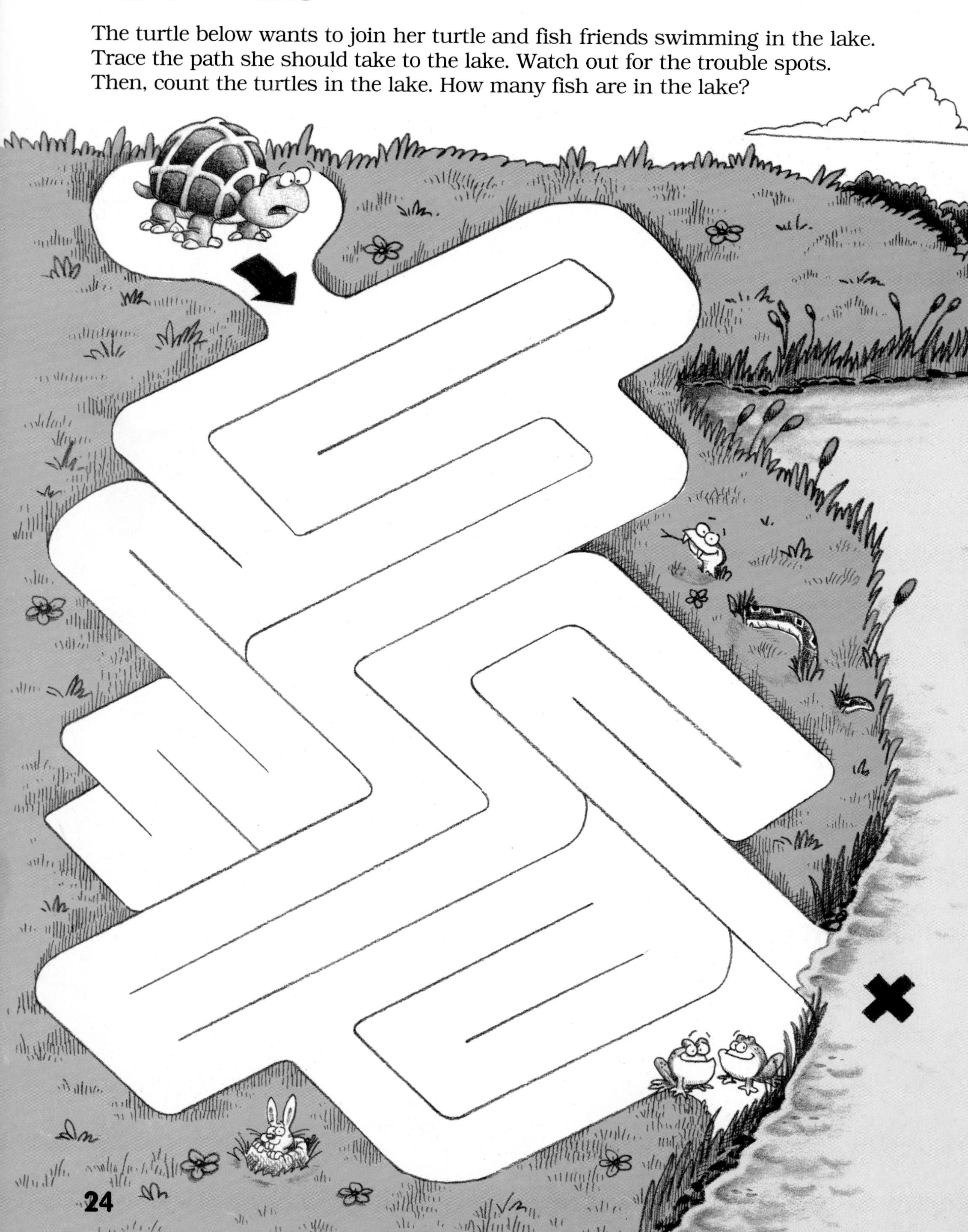

Paper-Plate Turtle

When exploring a lake, Max likes to keep his eyes to the ground. That's how he spotted these colorful turtles. How many colors can you put on your turtle?

What you'll need...

- Crayons or markers
- Construction paper
- Scissors
- One 6- or 7-inch flexible paper plate
- Tape
- One 3x5-inch index card, cut into four 1½x2½-inch pieces
- Construction paper, gift wrap, or magazine pages
- White crafts glue

1 Draw a turtle head on construction paper. For a turtle tail, draw a triangle. Cut out the head and the tail (see photo).

Fold the paper plate in half. Press the fold firmly with your fingers. Unfold the plate.

2 Tape the head to the inside of the plate, just above the fold. Tape the tail to the other side, just above the fold and inside the plate. Press the paper plate together on the fold and tape shut.

For toes and feet, draw 3 lines on each index card piece. Tape 2 feet to each side of the paper plate along the fold (see photo).

3 For the turtle shell, tear construction paper into small squares. Apply a dab of glue to the paper plate. Firmly press a paper square onto the glue (see photo). Keep gluing squares onto the paper plate till the plate is completely covered.

To make the turtle stand up, make a fold on each foot right next to the shell.

Nell the Turtle

I know a nice turtle named Nell
Who owns such a pretty shell
But, she walks oh so slow
'Cause her home she does tow
That if she is moving, who can tell?

Floating Fish

Splish! Splash! Assemble this water-loving fish and take it for a swim in a pool or your bathtub.

What you'll need...

- 2 plastic-foam plates or meat trays
- White crafts glue
- 2 buttons
- Scissors
- 1 waxed-paper or plastic-foam cup
- Crafts knife

1 For the fish body, place 1 plastic-foam plate on your work surface. Put glue on the rim. Place the other plate upside down on top of the first (see photo). For eyes, glue 1 button on each plate. Let dry for 5 minutes.

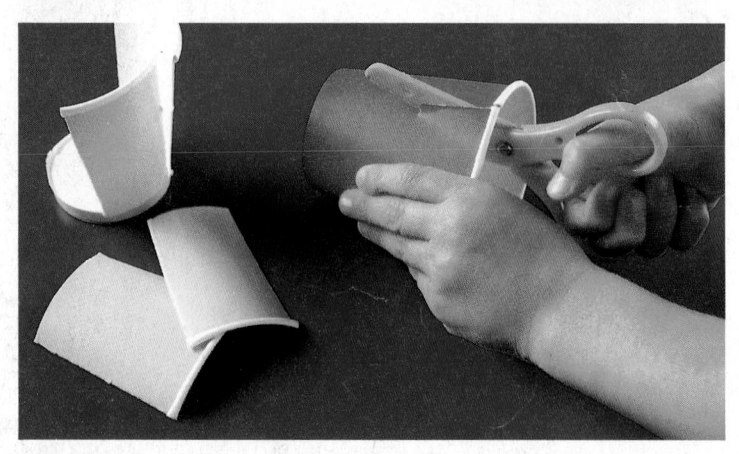

2 For the fins and tail, cut 4 slits in the paper cup, cutting from the top of the cup to the bottom (see photo). Cut the sides of the paper cup from the bottom. You should have 4 pieces. Throw the bottom away.

3 With adult help, use the crafts knife to cut slits in the fish body. In the top of the fish, cut 1 slit for a back fin. Then, cut 1 slit on each side in the middle of the fish. Cut another slit for the tail.

Push the fins and tail into the slits (see photo).

Fish Fins

If you make the fish fins and tail from a waxed paper cup, your fish may need new ones after a swim. Make the fins and tail as shown on page 28. Throw the old ones away. Push the new fins and tail into the slits in the fish. Now your fish is ready for another swim.

The Wonderful Woods

See pages 4 and 5

Children are fascinated by all kinds of animals and their homes. The animal homes shown on pages 4 and 5 are an anthill, a bird's nest, a rabbit burrow, a squirrel's nest, a spiderweb, and a beaver lodge.

Take a walk with your youngsters and look for animal homes. Even if you live in the city, you can find many animal homes such as an anthill, a bird's nest, a squirrel's nest, or a spider web.

Explain to your children that animals' homes should never be disturbed. It's dangerous to bother resting animals or animals with babies. Also, explain that animals have a right to live peacefully just like people do.

Woodsy Picture Frame

See pages 6 and 7

Our kid-testers had lots of ideas for pictures to frame. One little girl wanted to frame a photograph of herself to give to her mother. Other children preferred to draw pictures.

Once your children have completed the picture frames, they can do many things with them. In the photograph *(above, right)* the picture was glued to an inexpensive cardboard pencil box. Your children can stow their favorite possessions in these treasure chests.

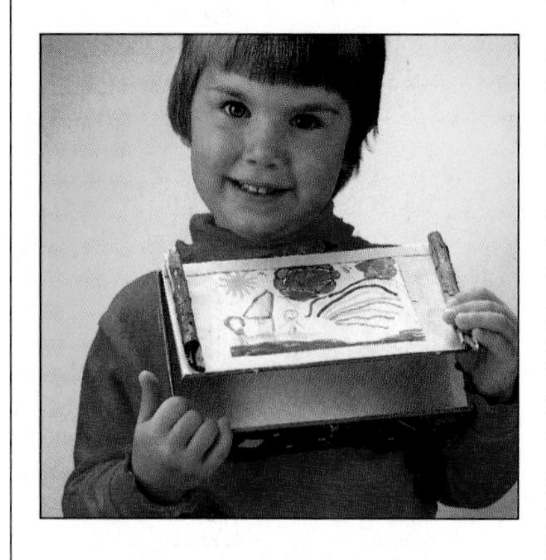

To hang the picture, tape the ends of a piece of string or yarn to the back of the picture.

For a stand-up picture frame, cut a piece of cardboard twice the size of the picture. Fold the cardboard in half and glue the picture to 1 side. The cardboard serves as a stand for the picture.

Cinnamon Snail Snacks

See pages 8 and 9

Here's some snail trivia to read to your children as they roll and dip these snail-shaped snacks:

- Snails live all over the world in woods, lakes, ponds, rivers, and oceans.

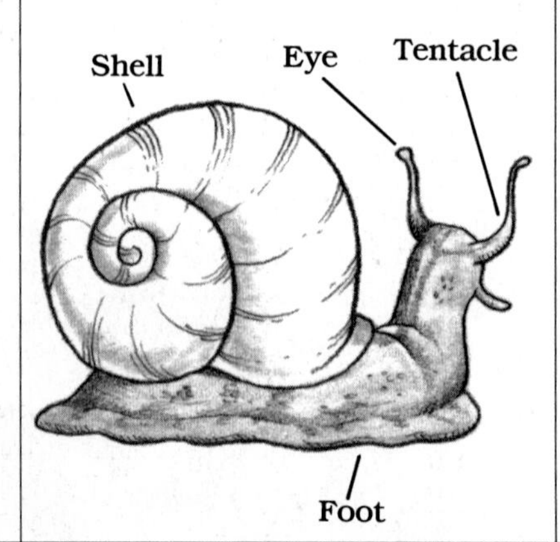

- In the woods, look for snails in moist places. Turn over leaves, stones, or logs.
- A snail has 1 foot. The foot is also the snail's stomach. This is the soft portion of the snail under the shell.
- To walk, a snail deposits a slimy substance in front of its foot. Then the snail slides over the slime.

Leaf Knickknack

See pages 10 and 11

The white clay for this project is perfect for use in many projects because it can be molded into just about any shape.

You will need to make the clay and cool it before your children use it. Since the clay keeps for several weeks if it is tightly wrapped in the refrigerator, you can make it ahead of time.

Homemade Clay

1 cup cornstarch
1 1-pound box baking soda
1½ cups water

- In a large saucepan mix cornstarch and baking soda. Gradually add water. Cook the mixture over low heat, stirring occasionally. The mixture will get bubbly, then thicken. Stir constantly until the mixture forms a ball.
- Remove from heat. Use a wooden spoon to transfer the clay to plastic wrap or foil. It will thicken as it cools. Cool completely. Tightly wrap any unused clay in plastic wrap and refrigerate.
- Bring clay to room temperature before using it.

Mountain Adventures

See pages 12 and 13

This activity helps your children learn the concept of pairs. A pair of skis, ski poles, boots, and mittens are among the hidden items in the picture on pages 12 and 13.

Ask your children to name other items that come in pairs. Some examples are earrings, socks, galoshes, slippers, tennis shoes, knitting needles, cymbals, and drumsticks .

Mud Mountain

See pages 14 and 15

Although our Homemade Mud is colored with cocoa powder and smells chocolaty, you won't want to eat it because it contains so much salt. But, if your children should sample some, it won't harm them. It's the salt that preserves the finished project. (For an edible chocolate treat, see Muddy Fudge, *above, right.*)

Homemade Mud

- 1 cup all-purpose flour
- ½ cup salt
- ⅓ cup unsweetened cocoa powder
- ½ cup water

- In a large mixing bowl stir together flour, salt, and cocoa powder. Add water. Stir till the flour mixture is moistened.
- Use a wooden spoon to transfer the dough to a lightly floured surface. Knead 10 minutes or till smooth.
- Place dough in a clear plastic bag. Store in the refrigerator.
- Before using the dough, check its consistency. If the dough is too sticky, knead in a small amount of flour. If the dough is too stiff, knead in several drops of water.

Muddy Fudge

This creamy chocolate fudge is the color of mud but is guaranteed to taste much better.

- In a small saucepan melt one 6-ounce package *semisweet chocolate pieces* over low heat.
- Meanwhile, use a table knife to cut two 3-ounce packages *cream cheese* into small pieces. Put the cream cheese in a large mixing bowl.
- Gradually stir in 2 cups sifted *powdered sugar* and 1 teaspoon *vanilla;* mix well.
- Add the melted chocolate pieces, 2 more cups of sifted *powdered sugar,* and, if desired, ½ cup chopped *nuts.* Stir until the mixture is creamy.
- Spread the mixture in a buttered 8x8x2-inch baking pan, patting with your fingers, if necessary. Cover and chill 2 hours or till firm. Cut into 1-inch squares. Store in the refrigerator. Makes 1¼ pounds (64 pieces).

Skis and Snow

See pages 16 and 17

Fluffy cotton becomes imaginary snow for these tiny skis. Here's another fun project that uses cotton for snow. Ask your children to draw a winter picture. Then, wherever they want snow in the picture, they can glue cotton balls.

Desert Fun

See pages 18 and 19

Even children too young to spell can find the items that begin with the letter S. Explain that all the items begin with the same sound. Mention several words that begin with S, such as sad, special, and Sunday. Ask them to find the objects in the picture that begin with the same sound as these words.

Sew-and-Stuff Cactus

See pages 20 and 21

Cacti are fascinating plants because they need little water to survive. Explain to your children that cacti grow in the desert where other plants would die from lack of moisture. Here are some of the reasons why:

- After it rains, the roots of a cactus absorb water. The cactus stores water in its stem.
- The ribbed surface of the cactus allows it to expand after a rainfall when the stem fills up with water. This water may need to last the plant an entire year. As the plant uses the water, the stem becomes smaller.
- The outside of a cactus is thick and waxy. This prevents water loss.
- A cactus doesn't have any leaves. Leaves require too much moisture for plants to live in the desert.
- Purchase a cactus and show your children the water-saving characteristics of the plant.

Rigatoni Rattlesnake

See pages 22 and 23

Before your children start to make snakes, you will need to draw Rattlesnake Tails on construction paper. (See pattern, *right.*) Draw the fold lines on the tail.

For a more colorful snake, dye the rigatoni. Here's how: Fill a bowl with cold water and add a few drops of food coloring. (Blue and red food coloring give the best results.) Add the rigatoni to the water. Let stand 15 minutes. Pour off the water. Spread the colored rigatoni on waxed paper. Let dry about 6 hours.

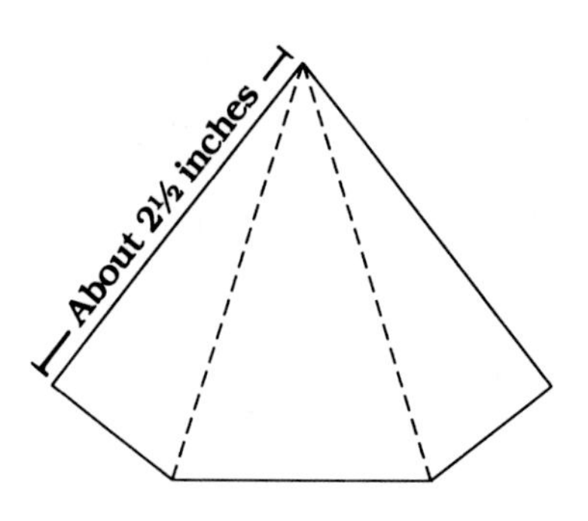

Lake Pals

See pages 24 and 25

While your children have fun solving this maze, tell them about turtles.

- Turtles belong to a group of animals called reptiles. Lizards and snakes also are reptiles.

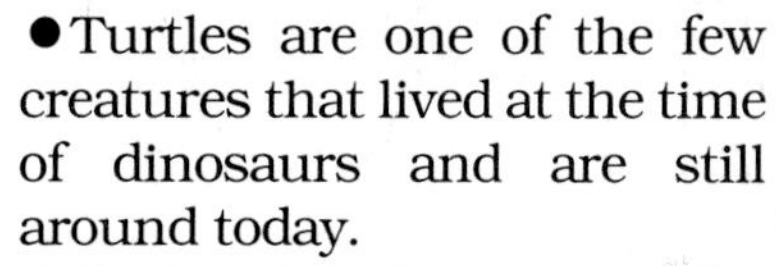

- Turtles are one of the few creatures that lived at the time of dinosaurs and are still around today.
- Turtles live in or near the water. A tortoise is similar to a turtle, but lives on land and seldom goes into water.
- Turtles live longer than most other animals. Some live to be more than 100 years old.

Paper-Plate Turtle

See pages 26 and 27

Some of our kid-testers wanted to glue the paper squares to both sides of the turtle. Others were content with decorating just 1 side. Your children can use crayons to draw squares on the paper plate instead of gluing on the paper squares.

If you don't have a paper plate, just trace a 6-inch circle on a piece of heavy paper or cardboard. Cut out the circle and fold it in half as you would the paper plate.

Floating Fish

See pages 28 and 29

Here are some fish facts to share with your children:

- You use your lungs to breath, but fish have gills instead of lungs.
- Fish have ears inside their heads so you can't see them.
- Fish don't have eyelids so they can never close their eyes.
- Fish swim in groups called schools.

BETTER HOMES AND GARDENS® BOOKS
Art Director: Ernest Shelton Managing Editor: David A. Kirchner
Family Life Editor: Sharyl Heiken

LET'S GO EXPLORING
Editors: Sandra Granseth and Mary Major Williams Graphic Designers: Mick Schnepf and Linda Vermie
Project Manager: Liz Anderson
Contributing Illustrator: Buck Jones
Contributing Photographer: Scott Little